The Other Side of Thru

Payne Nickerson

A New Day Publishing
Atlanta

THE OTHER SIDE OF THRU BY PAYNE NICKERSON

This book is a work of fiction. Names, characters, places and incidents either are products of the author's imagination or are used fictitiously. Any resemblance to actual events or locales or persons, living or dead, is entirely coincidental.

Copyright © 2013 by Payne Nickerson

All rights reserved. Except as permitted under the U.S Copyright Act of 1976, no part of this publication may be reproduced, distributed, or transmitted in any form or by any means, or stored in a database or retrieval system, without the prior written permission of the author, except for the inclusion of brief quotations in a review.

Soft Cover Edition

ISBN 978-0-9899280-0-7

First Edition 2013.

Printed in the United States of America.

Other side of Thru by Payne Nickerson

Published by: A New Day Publishing
www.anewdaybooks.com

THE OTHER SIDE OF THRU BY PAYNE NICKERSON

THE OTHER SIDE OF THRU BY PAYNE NICKERSON

PREFACE

This work was inspired by a very talented television/film writer and great friend of mine, Adolpha Cole, who told me years ago that my life story and experiences are worth sharing. She stated that it is powerful and will give hope to others that they can overcome any obstacle, become successful and happy. It is my hope that despite our tendency as people to read for entertainment and for the ability to gossip, people will read my story with an eye of appreciation for God's grace and mercy. It is my hope that some young person or woman who is unsure of her future and if God hears her prayers will read this and know, yes…He hears you and has not forgotten you. My life and its circumstances are still a work in progress. I know that God has more for me to do and accomplish

THE OTHER SIDE OF THRU BY PAYNE NICKERSON

The writing and completion of this work was imperative to the times in which we live. I give a general overview of my life situations and circumstances (in themes not in chronological order), without going into gory detail about the abuses that I have endured - thus giving glory to those who have abused me. I do not demonize any of the people who have mistreated me. I only give my account of the happenings and how they have shaped my life, faith and value system. Each person has their own version of happenings, but God knows the truth and I am here sharing with you my accounts, as they happened. There are many who have inspired me to complete this work and who have supported my vision for the reach of this book. I would like to thank my sisters, my son, and my friends for pushing me to write, even when I doubted that anyone would "get it". I would also like to thank Cassandra for introducing me to the owners of A

THE OTHER SIDE OF THRU BY PAYNE NICKERSON

New Day Publishing, because she believes in the work and felt like the story needed to be told in order to inspire others. Sonia and Jarvis, my best friends overall, your unconditional love, encouragement and inside jokes have helped me to be ready to endure all that will come with being "naked and unashamed". To A New Day Publishing staff and owners, THANK YOU.

To the man that God has for me, I know you will read this work and have more appreciation and love for me than ever before. I know that you will see my life experiences as a testament to strength, courage and love, and that your love for me is as deep, pure and loyal as my love for you, without condition.

For those who abused me, judged me, and did everything in their power to break me...THANK YOU. I am the sum total of my experiences and God gets the glory.

DEDICATION

This book is dedicated to my Sun, who inspires me to be as strong, willful and tenacious as he is. You have a great calling upon your life. I am proud to share my story, along with the beginning of yours, I am humbly honored to be the vessel God used to bring you into life.

This book is also dedicated to all of the young women who have fallen victim to statistics and society's expectations of you based on your past. God says you are worthy. And I am a living testimony that WE are worthy of all that is meant for our highest and greatest good.

THE OTHER SIDE OF THRU BY PAYNE NICKERSON

TABLE OF CONTENTS

Chapter One – Life Ain't No Crystal Stair

Chapter Two – The Path Less Traveled

Chapter Three – Friends and Family

Chapter Four – Sojourning to find MY Truth

Chapter Five – Freedom in Forgiveness

Chapter Six – Accepting the Gift of Goodbye

Chapter Seven – Phoenix: And Still I Rise

A Return to Love by Marianne Williamson

Risk by Anais Nin

Chapter 1
Life Ain't No Crystal Stair

Life for me ain't been no crystal stair.
It's had tacks in it,
And splinters,
And boards torn up,
And places with no carpet on the floor --
Bare.
- *Langston Hughes, Mother to Son*

"Payne, get away from that gate!" she yelled, as I kicked and screamed and cried out, "I want my sisters!" She was Deborah, the daycare provider, and I hated her. I screamed, cried and reached out. Only the dividing gate kept me from running to my older sisters. Did they know? Could they know that I spent my days being beaten with a belt that I vividly remember 35 years later? It was a clear plastic belt that was torn at the buckle end and gave a sharp sting when it hit my unbruised skin. The pain was vivid. And with each sting, I could hear Deborah yell, "You are going to sit there until you eat your lunch!!" Lunch every day at Deborah's was spaghetti-Os. I began to hate spaghetti-Os (the smell of them still makes me nauseous to this day).Many days I fell asleep at the table, having not finished my lunch, and was awakened to a piercing sting across my back like the whip against Kunta's back in the movie *Roots*. The unforgettable pain would embed abuse into my psyche. It became a daily dance of ours until one fateful day.

"Payne, what is wrong?" asked my mother. As usual, I responded "Nothing, I am fine". I had become withdrawn and sick. My mother sensed something was wrong and had gone awry. She looked at me sternly, in my eyes and asked again, "Baby girl, what is wrong with you?" And with fear and tears, I said again,

"Nothing". Upon removing my clothing, I saw her cringe and her face turned red. I knew I was in trouble. She called for my father to come see. He saw. turned, leaned in and asked, "Baby girl, what happened to you?" I hunched my three year old shoulders, looked him in his face and said, "I don't know, Daddy".

My sisters gathered around and speak of how Deborah acted, would treat us badly and kept us separated. My mother jumped up and grabbed the phone. I heard her soft voice turn stern and firm to say, "My children will not be returning and you will hear from our lawyer!" I knew it was serious. That night, my bath water felt as if it were salt water washing across my wounds. Each sting brought a tear and an "ouch!" I then noticed in the mirror while my sister was dressing me that I had big red whelps from the belt beating I had endured. But there were also small black spots as a result of Deborah's cigarettes placed upon my skin to punish me. After that, my parents never put me in daycare again but I had been scarred for life. And it set the precedence for a life of abuse and still replying "Nothing" often when asked what the problem is or what happened to me.

To understand my journey you have to understand my family dynamics. I am the youngest of five girls in a blended family situation. I was named for my father and definitely the apple of his eye. My dad was home during the day and worked nights when my parents were married. He combed my hair, watched Sesame Street with me daily, a taught me the alphabet and how to tie my shoes. I remember him often crying because things weren't right. He oftentimes walked to get us food because we hadn't been fed. Mom was always at work. He also walked us to school to ensure our safety. As times got tougher economically, my parents were hard hit.

THE OTHER SIDE OF THRU BY PAYNE NICKERSON

Fast-forward eleven years and once again I was replying that "nothing was wrong". My sister, Sabrina was speaking to my mom and I could hear them in hushed voices from my room. "Mom, I think Payne is sick and you should take her to the doctor", said Sabrina. My mom, in her typical not wanting to miss work fashion, stated "I don't have time to take her to the doctor. I have to work". Sabrina replied, "Trust me, you should take her. She is not well". Later the next day, we rode in the car to the doctor's appointment in complete silence. The tension in the car was so thick you could slice it.

I slowly approached the cold and deserted looking white building that was filled with local teens. I shrank down in my seat, hoping none of the busy teens would talk to me or ask why I was there. It was crowded, hot and packed. I picked up one of the many brochures that addressed all types of health problems and I pretended to read it. All the while thinking, she (my mother) is going to kill me. I looked towards both exit doors and my heart was pounding so fast I could hear each beat. I began to feel dizzy, nauseous and panicked. Right when I felt as if I was going to pass out, I heard someone say, "Payne Nickerson...Payne Nickerson". It was the nurse.

I felt as if I was taking the long walk to judgment as I followed her into an examination room. I walked into the sterile, pristine room with vaginal and penis models, body charts on the wall, and all types of tools that look liked our 9th grade science dissection kits. I kept pretending not to know the obvious. I was pregnant. But I had more fear of my mother's anger than of giving birth and becoming a mom. I was fourteen years old and had just completed my first semester of my 9th grade year of high school. I was lost, alone, rejected by my peers and wanted so badly to be loved by someone, something. I believed that I'd have someone who would love me unconditionally, something I'd never known or felt.

    I sighed heavily when the nurse returned from the lab and I pretended to be shocked when she said, "Your uterus is larger than normal, you are pregnant and due in August". "Do you have anyone here with you? If not, we can discuss your options and you can decide later", the nurse said. I replied, "My mother is in the waiting room but I can't tell her. You don't understand, she's going to kill me". She called my mother into the examination room and I proceeded to cry. Right then and there I wished for some natural disaster to happen and interrupt the news.

The nurse turned and said, "Ms. Nickerson, Payne is pregnant and she is due in August. There are multiple options for her and I have given her brochures to read over with you. Since she is 14 and a minor, she will need your permission for whatever she does. I have also given her condoms for future use". My mother was shocked but more embarrassed than anything else. She turned to me and just shook her head in disappointment. We stood, thanked the nurse and walked to the car in silence. When we got to the car she asked, "When did this happen? Where were you? Who is the father?" I began to cry harder, "the father?" I had not thought about him or his reaction. Fear grew in my heart, loneliness filled my space, as I shrank into the car seat and held my stomach to say, "It's my choice". We rode the rest of the way home to our Atlanta suburb living space and I went straight to my room. I walked past two of my sisters and said nothing.

THE OTHER SIDE OF THRU BY PAYNE NICKERSON

As I sat on my bed in my cold and quiet room, my sister Kisa came in and said, "What's wrong?", as usual, I replied "Nothing". I am the youngest daughter, the one who was not allowed to do anything. Oftentimes my family members boasted and bragged about my grades and intellect and how much of a good girl I was. I felt as if I had failed them all. My mother stood in the doorway of my bedroom and said in an angry voice, "I ought to throw this lamp at you. What were you thinking? Who is this boy?" She then walked to her room and proceeded to call my father. My parents had been divorced for nine years but my dad was still active in our lives. She walked back into my room and said, "Your father is upset. He doesn't even want to talk to you. Tell me who this boy is and where you were when you got pregnant". I still told her nothing but his name. He was an older man, a college student from a well-known Atlanta family and I was a

14 year old from the "wrong side of the tracks". What she didn't know was I had told him a month earlier and he threatened me, called me a "hoe" and said it wasn't his child. He said that I was trying to trap him.

The question was, trap him for what? Terrence was a college student with no income. His family was not wealthy nor was he an athlete. We met earlier that summer at a mutual friend's 16th birthday party. I was a virgin and had just lost a boyfriend (whom I later married) because I wasn't ready for sex. Months into the 'relationship' we had sex after he gave me an ultimatum and I didn't want to lose another boyfriend. The second sexual encounter resulted in my pregnancy. And that one decision would dictate the course of my entire life.

THE OTHER SIDE OF THRU BY PAYNE NICKERSON

My mother contacted my child's father. They decided an abortion was best. I did everything in my power to avoid an abortion, and eventually I did. Terrence was livid that I told his father that I was pregnant. He tortured me with threats and verbal abuse during my entire pregnancy. He then began to feign interest in being a father. I felt confused and suspicious of his sudden interest in the baby, the position of the baby and my exact due date. He called one day and asked my mother if he could take me to a movie and she said yes. He arrived dressed in Adidas head to toe with a new watch and new tennis shoes.

We left and it began to rain. It was one of the worst thunderstorms the city had ever seen. We could barely see out of the truck windows. The streets were flooded and cars were splashing water from the street onto other car windshields. I began to get a knot in my stomach and feel nauseous. He then said, "We aren't going to make the movie in this weather. We have to pull over". I said, "Ok". We pulled over into a parking lot that looked like it was attached to a baseball park and we sat there for a minute. The wind howled and the lightning grew quicker. The storm was getting stronger and closer to where we were.

He said, "We should get out of the car and get under the shelter ahead of us". I declined. He scooted closer to me in the truck and kissed me and said, "Come on, this storm is bad and we are safer under the shelter than in this truck". I reluctantly got out of the truck and did a light jog with him to the covered tables at the park. We were soaked. As I stood there, Terrence kissed me again and said we would wait there until the storm calmed down. He said, "Tell me again where the baby is". I took his hand and placed it on my stomach and showed him where his son's head was positioned. I smiled as it seemed he was really interested and had a genuine change of heart.

He pulled me in for a kiss and as I leaned back to say something to him I felt someone grab me from behind. I started fighting for my life. I could see Terrence in front of me while I was fighting. Whomever my male attacker was seemed slightly taller than me and wore glasses because at some point I knocked them off. I felt a cloth over my nose and tried my best not to inhale. I kept fighting. I finally snatched the cloth from my attacker and threw it but he never let me go. Then I couldn't see anything. It was jet black but I was still pressed against his chest. I felt the cloth back over my nose and looked around; there was no sign of Terrence in front of me, on the ground or otherwise. I began to feel weak and as I fought not to go to sleep.

THE OTHER SIDE OF THRU BY PAYNE NICKERSON

I saw an apparition of my uncle in a minister's white robe. My uncle had been killed years earlier in a robbery and I always thought of him as my angel. Once I saw him, I gave in to the cold dark night. I knew that I would be alright, no matter which side I woke up on, here or heaven. As I began to pass out and fall to the ground, I remember saying, "my baby". I am unsure of how much time passed while I was out, but when I came to the storm had subsided. I opened my eyes and Terrence lay there on the ground. I reached out to wake him up and he jumped up. Our appearance was opposite; I was muddy and looked like I had been in the fight of my life. He was still clean and looking like he was fresh out of an Adidas ad. We began to run towards his truck.

He said, "I got hit in the head pretty badly". I tried to glance at his head but it was on the opposite side he pointed to so I couldn't see anything. He said,

"You want to go to my dorm and get cleaned up". That statement baffled me because I thought victims of crime should go to the police. My instinct kicked in and I said, "No, I want to go home". He drove me back home and Kisa opened the door. Her face looked as if she had seen a ghost. She yelled, "Mama! Come here!!" My mother came running downstairs and her mouth fell open when she laid eyes upon me. My sister asked Terrence, "What happened?" In his own words, he replayed the event and told her that he'd been knocked out and hit in the head with something on the right side of his head. I frowned. That was the opposite side of the side he told me in the truck. I looked at my sister wide eyed, like a deer in headlights and I proceeded to walk upstairs to my room.

    My sister and I left him to talk to my mom. I did not want to go back down there because I could not fathom that anyone would do such a thing. I asked myself: Have I been set up? Did he do this? Why was I dirty and he was clean? Why does he keep changing the side of his head he got hit on? Who gave the cloth back to my attacker? He never let me go. I heard the door downstairs close. He was gone. My mother came rushing upstairs and started her own investigation before calling my doctors to get me an appointment.

    Slowly I walked down the hall to the bathroom to wash up. I looked into the mirror and began to cry. My hair was disheveled, my face bloody and peeling around the nose and mouth, my clothes muddy and torn. But the worst part was when I opened my jacket, there were shoe prints all over the stomach part of my shirt and thigh part of my pants. I had been kicked, beaten and at the insistence of my doctor, raped. I fell to the cold bathroom tile and began to cry, I just lay there. Kisa came in to comfort me, to bathe me and help me get into the bed. I was 15 years old. I began to wonder, How did I get here? Why me? What about my son? Would he survive such an attack? Would I ever be able to sleep or trust gain? I was devastated, scared and thinking this is something out of a made for TV movie.

The attacker took nothing from him, not his fancy watch, car or wallet. They took everything from me...my sense of security, trust, innocence, and for years my ability to sleep or not be afraid of the dark. For years, I would fight in my sleep often and awaken to a scratched up face, suffering from PTSD.

For the remainder of my pregnancy I avoided Terrence. I didn't take calls, make calls, or see him. My teachers and coaches 'watched' me after school (he'd attempted to check me out before). I was seeing the school psychologist, friends shunned me, and some teachers just looked disappointed. I kept going. But the anonymous calls kept coming. Daily, someone called playing Sade's "Smooth Operator" whenever I answered the phone. To this day I cannot hear her music without cringing.

Two weeks before the start of my sophomore year in high school I gave birth to a healthy baby boy. My mother called Terrence to let him and his parents know about the baby. She was promptly cursed out and told to find the real daddy because Terrence was not the father. I told her leave them alone. I wanted nothing to do with him and was terrified to have to deal with him again. When I returned home with my son, our electricity had been turned back on and it gave me hope for a better and brighter future. Terrence's parents reached out to my mother via my aunt and arranged to come by our home to see the baby and me.

Upon walking in, they had cases of milk and pampers and greeted us very nicely but suspicious. Terrence's mother introduced herself and asked, "How did you meet my son?" I answered her. Coldly, she stated, "Terrence has told us that you are his friend and he was trying to help you and now you are trying to blame this baby on him". I just shook my head and told her, "I was a virgin prior to meeting your son. I am 110% sure that this is his son". I looked at Terrence's father and said, "You know this is his baby".

It was clear that there were things Terrence and his father shared that his mother did not know. I had spoken to Terrence's father during my pregnancy and he never denied the baby to his father, but that was between them. While Terrence's mom and I were playing 20 questions, his father was playing with the baby. After all of her questions, she asked to hold my son. I let her hold him and she loved him immediately just like his grandfather had and always has. His grandfather was immediately drawn to him and their bond remains to this very day. They handed my mother some money before leaving, offered to find out paternity and if their grandchild, they would raise him. Of course, they saw how we were living and wanted to give him better but my son was my responsibility and I didn't trust his father to be anywhere near him. I'd die first. And I almost had.

Postpartum, I had a lot of time to think as I was waiting for school to start. As I lay there in pain from natural childbirth and post-delivery surgery, I had to come to terms with many things. How did I get here? Why sex so early? Absentee father? Yes. Low self-esteem? Yes. Fearing rejection and not being loved? Yes. All of these questions had me thinking about my past and my true first sexual encounters. I was battling with whether or not I was gay because my first sexual encounter at the age of four was with my mother and father's best female friend.

My parents had vowed to never put me in daycare again and entrusted their female best friend to watch me during the day while my mother worked and my father rested and ran errands. She would wait every day until the news came on and talk to the TV news anchor and say, "Oh Monica, you a bad girl. I wish I could be with you". She often times would stop and lift her head from between my legs to watch TV and to shake her head at the news and the things going on in the world. This happened on more than one occasion. Whenever my dad was about to pick me up, she would say, "Remember, it's our game and your mom and dad said we could play". One day I got into the car with my dad and said, "Daddy, we played a game". He was ignoring me. I said again, "Daddy, we played a game". And his response was, "Yeah, yeah honey, you played a game. That's good". So I looked out the window at the trees and the houses and remained quiet for eleven years about 'the game'.

A year later at the age of five, my parents divorced and mom couldn't afford day care; I would spend the day with my stepfather. We would watch Sesame Street, play games and eat lunch together each day. One day I was sitting on his lap and gave him a big hug for the cookie he gave me. When I pulled back from the hug, he kissed me. That kiss led to many kisses and to my surprise he slipped his tongue in my mouth. I tried to pull back but he held me tighter and straddled me across his lap. I could feel the bulge in his pants and it scared me. I felt that this was wrong. It continued to happen and oftentimes afterwards he would give me more cookies and looks as if I better not tell. I feared him so much so that I would beg my friends to stay over or not go home because I did not want to be alone with him. These experiences molded my beliefs about love, sex and trust. So in my confusion, I often had sex with men out of fear they would take it anyway or to gain love. This erroneous thinking would take years to undo. Years later I would confide in my older sisters and my mother. My mother was surprised at his actions with me although she knew he had been accused of being "inappropriate" with one of his nieces.

I often refer to my son's birth as my own. It forced me to confront my past and to begin a long journey on the road to healing. I often tell people, he gave birth to me. He gave me purpose. Before him, I felt alone, sad and suicidal because of my past. Although many of my peers shunned me and tried to make me ashamed for being pregnant at 14 and a mother at 15, I believe with all my heart, his life saved my own. God entrusted me with this beautiful being and I prayed everyday over him. I believe that his life has purpose and I gave him a unique name to bear because there would be no other like him before or after. Oftentimes I tell him, he is my air. And our bond would become stronger as he watched me struggle through high school, college, a failed marriage, bad relationships, money hardships and as I watched him fight for his life that fateful winter of 2011.

THE OTHER SIDE OF THRU BY PAYNE NICKERSON

Chapter 2
The Path Less Traveled

I shall be telling this with a sigh
Somewhere ages and ages hence:
Two roads diverged in a wood, and I—
I took the one less traveled by,
And that has made all the difference.
Robert Frost, 1920, The Road Not Taken

"Brrrrnnnnnggggggg!!" Like clockwork, I roll out of bed and stumble to the bathroom to turn on the light and reach for my face cloth. The bathroom tile is cold and I am groggy from being up late doing homework. I hear my mom in her bathroom getting dressed and I hear little feet running down the hallway towards my bathroom. The door slowly opens and a little head peaks in smiling wide with those big eyes that melt my heart into pieces. A tiny voice says, "Hey mommy!!" I laugh and respond, "Hey Bean!" He stands there in his Grover feet pajamas waiting for me to unzip him. I unzip him and put him on his potty. He watches me get dressed as he sits there and when he's done we celebrate, "Yaaayy!" Then I can hear my mom yelling down the hallway for me to check his daycare bag while she finishes dressing him. So I check his Sesame Street bag for the necessary items and I check my backpack for my homework. I sigh heavily and we pack up in my mom's car to be dropped off at daycare and high school. It is my senior year and it is turbulent. I am in several AP classes, active in student organizations, applying to colleges, preparing to take the SAT, and prayerful about a scholarship. I am still in the top of my class but my ranking has dropped since having my son because the balance of it all was a bit much at times.

THE OTHER SIDE OF THRU BY PAYNE NICKERSON

"Hey Payne!" yelled out my friend Tee. "Girl that AP Calculus homework was a monster, did you finish it?" I tell her, "Yes, I finished it but I have to stay after school today to complete a make-up test that I missed when Bean was sick". I know what it all means, so without hesitation, I reach into my locker and give her my AP Cal folder. I then tell her meet me before class on third hall to give it back before we go into class. She smiles, winks and walks away. Shortly thereafter, I feel a hand on my back and a voice says, "You coming to the game this weekend?" It is him. He is an athletic star at my high school. He is tall dark, handsome and super smart. I had the biggest crush on him but he had a reputation for using girls and never had an interest in me until I had a baby. I respond, "No, I can't come, I don't have a sitter". That was a lie. My mom and sisters would sit for me if I asked; however, I tried hard not to ask too often. Besides, I had a boyfriend and was committed because he was ok with me having a son. I moved slowly past Mr. Wonderful Ball Player, smiled and went into my AP English class.

I sat alone in that class. I was an outcast because I was poor, didn't have the best clothes and my hair was often in a ponytail to hide the need for a relaxer touch up. I went into class. sat and watched the other girls talk about shopping, dates, college and hanging out after school. No one invited me. Class started and I barely participated because my mind was elsewhere. I was still upset with Terrence over our son. I was trying to do my best in school. I was a social outcast but popular because I was intelligent and friendly. And I was fighting to be better so that my son could have better. My mind drifted as we reviewed *Hamlet* and *Who's Afraid of Virginia Wolf?* After class my teacher handed me a note and said that he and his wife looked up some services that may be of assistance to me. I looked at the yellow sticky note and it had the number to the Department of Family and Children Services (DFACS) on it. I smiled because I knew he meant well, but also was perplexed because how could someone so knowledgeable not know that DFACS was of no benefit to someone like me? That they would be more of a hindrance than a help? That they'd get all up in our family business and I didn't need that kind of problem.

As soon as I exited the classroom, I threw the yellow piece of paper in the nearest trash can. After school, I headed back up the lonely hallway to take my AP Cal exam that I'd missed. Mrs. Heathers said, "Payne, you have missed a lot of days this school year and I am going to have to call the social worker". I sat there and cried. Then she inquired, "What is going on with you? You seem distant. Your homework has crayon all over it. And you keep missing school". I sighed and told her I would tell her after I completed my exam. Once I finished the exam, I said "Mrs. Heathers, I have a two year old son and that is who draws on my AP homework, I apologize. He's been very ill with an ear infection and I have to stay home with him because he couldn't go to daycare until his fever was gone for 24 hours. So when I am sick or he is, I have to stay home. He is my kid and my mom can't miss work because we have to have her income". She looked at me with the saddest eyes and said, "Well we will have to figure something out." I told her of my earlier experience with my AP English teacher and she smiled and said, "Everyone doesn't know. He was really trying to help". I nodded in agreement and told her I had to go because I had to walk up to the daycare, pick up my son and meet my mom to ride home. I walked up the street to the daycare and went into Bean's class. He was playing and running around. He gave me the usual smile and bright eyed, "Hey Mommy!!" Funny, he is still bright eyed and a man of few words.

Bean was a smart and lively kid who loved drawing on my homework and pretending he had homework too. I was extremely protective of him with everyone and he still remains my Achilles heel. His grandparents were very involved in his life and so was his uncle, he is fortunate to have them. Terrence remained bitter and distant for a while. He would show up for all of our son's activities, he just was not a financially supportive father. Terrence's parents oftentimes paid his child support for him. Bean's grandparents were very encouraging of my education and participation in extracurricular activities. Oftentimes they paid for me to participate in activities.

THE OTHER SIDE OF THRU BY PAYNE NICKERSON

During my senior year, I applied to seven colleges and was accepted with partial to full rides to five of them. I was proud and dating whom I believed to be the love of my life, Xavier. He was accepting of my kid and my talents. Xavier, was a few years older, a tall brown brother with almond shaped eyes, dimples and well dressed. It was hard making the decision to leave them both and attend college out of state. But I had to go where the money was and where I felt I'd be most supported and successful. My freshman year was at a small town southern historically black college majoring in biology/pre-med. I had many friends, was dorm president and enjoyed college fully; but I struggled with my studies as they were often interrupted by drama at home. I had no source of income and could not call home for help. My mom had less than a high school education and no extra income. I could not afford my books so oftentimes I borrowed others' books. I had to read and do my homework late hours after everyone else had completed theirs. I would end that freshman year with a 2.7 gpa based on having NO books and lose my scholarship because of it.

The drama at home didn't help either. I left for school with the understanding that my mother and one of my sisters would care for my son. I also left with the intent of completing my education without interruption as Bean's father had. Then the calls began. Bean's grandparents calling to say my mom won't let them see him. My mom calling to say they're stiffing her on child support. And my sister (a new college grad) saying you wouldn't like how things are going, I am doing the best I can. I cried a lot but I knew an education was the only way out. Then the call came...

THE OTHER SIDE OF THRU BY PAYNE NICKERSON

I walked into the dorm and up four flights of stairs to my room and saw several missed calls messages on my board. The number did not look familiar so I ran down the hall to the pay phone to find out who had called six times. As I ran, I prayed, "Lord please let Bean be ok". The closer I got to the phone, the larger the knot in my stomach grew. I dialed the number and pressed extension 116. "Hello Department of Family and Children Services, Ms. Smith speaking", a nice voice said. I responded, "Hi, this is Payne Nickerson, and I have several missed calls from this number". "Hi Ms. Nickerson, your mother came in and filed for food stamps and welfare for your son". I started getting the knot in my stomach again. She went on and on about how I would have to transfer custody to my mother in order for her to get assistance for him. I did not understand what was going on. I politely exited my phone call with her and after several conversations with my sister, my mom and Terrence's parents I found out the real deal.

They were fighting over Bean, my mother said they weren't paying her the child support and they said she wouldn't let them see him. My sister said, "You need to come home, it's a mess". And I kept hearing Ms. Smith's words echoing in my head, "In the sight of the state of Georgia, you abandoned your son and did not leave him in anyone's guardianship". I sunk to the floor in the tiny phone booth. The small space folded me like an ironing board; but didn't conceal my crying as it echoed down the freshman hallway and began to garner attention. I thought to myself "HELL NO!!" My mom did the best she could but I couldn't let him grow up like me - abused, hungry, poor and put on the back burner (these judgments would haunt me later). I could not let him live with his grandparents, although they could provide, I honestly feared his safety around a father who after 3 years still had not "come around". So I went to the dean to ask for help. I'd been a promising student and was active on campus. But they didn't have family housing or a lot of options for "students in my position". Needless to say, I dropped out and returned home.

Upon returning home, mom was living with her long-term boyfriend. She stated we could stay for the summer but had to move. I was devastated. "Payne, you have to find somewhere to go" said my mom. I shook my head and said, "Where will I go? I don't have a job and only have one year of college education". She said, "I don't know but you have to find somewhere to go. There is no space for you all here and we want our privacy". I looked at my sister in disbelief. I said, "But you have helped all your other kids with their children when they were grown. I am trying to do something with myself. It's not like I am just laying up". She looked at me without flinching and turned her back and walked into her room and shut the door.

At that moment the doorbell rang. It was Xavier, my longtime boyfriend. Xavier had the strangest look on his face. I tried to feign happiness but I could tell he heard the entire conversation through the door. I smiled, grabbed Bean and out the door we went with Xavier to dinner. Later that month my sister, Vashti, went to live with church members. I scrambled to find somewhere for us to go in hopes that my son's grandparents would not find out and take him for good.

Although I knew Xavier had heard the conversation through the door I was still embarrassed to admit the truth to him about my home situation. He took us in and married me three months later at the insistence of his very religious family. I will preface this by stating that he was a good father. He was attentive and supportive to our son but not a good husband. Some people aren't meant for marriage and the long-term commitment to ONE person. He on paper and in person can be impressive, but when alcohol or women entered the situation, he was a different being. Someone I did not recognize.

I continued to take classes at a local state university, work part time at a day care, and be a mother and wife all at 19 years old. Xavier was a student and truck driver at the time. We started out with meager beginnings and tried build the normalcy that neither one of us had as children. Within a year we were buying a home in a nice Atlanta suburb and enrolling Bean in kindergarten. We regularly attended church, were active in the PTA, were sports boosters for our son's teams, and were supportive through his academic and talkative whoas. Xavier was a great father and he was very patient (more so than I). He never judged my past or the things that I had been through in my lifetime. I loved him dearly and thought I could not live without him. Life was good, so we thought.

It was difficult hiding the things we were going through. I oftentimes borrowed money from my family to meet basic needs. I felt inadequate as a wife because my earnings were barely helping him and he was working 14 hour days. At that time I was also dealing with having child support checks that bounced (intentionally). We were going back and forth in court with Bean's father and it proved daunting. Eventually it would take a toll on our relationship. I felt like a burden more than a wife and certain members of his family made sure I knew they had issue with it. I faced multiple problems with a sister in law that hated me and gave me grief at every turn.

We oftentimes had Sunday or holiday dinners with Xavier's grandmother, which would include his father, sister and cousins. The moment we walked in his sister would hug him and roll her eyes at me. She often times took jabs at me. If I was talkative she would say, "You are trying too hard". If I was quiet, she would say, "Oh Miss Thang thinks she better than everyone". But because they were left without their mother at a young age, they had a strong bond and they were all they had. I tried hard not to have beef with her or put Xavier in the middle.

THE OTHER SIDE OF THRU BY PAYNE NICKERSON

One summer she came to live with us and it was a trying time. I tried my best to stay on her good side and keep the tension down. We were sitting and watching a movie and I said, "Wow that was good. But I hate when people change when they are around others". She, at 16 years old, then said, "You act like that when you get around your sisters". Xavier sat there and said nothing, yet again. So I looked at her and said, "What? Girl please, I am myself all the time, I don't change when I get around my sisters. I am me all the time". We went back and forth for an hour and entered into a cursing match and he just walked upstairs to our bedroom and said nothing. She was crying and so was I. We were tired of fighting and she believed her brother was putting me first. He should have, I was his wife. I never tried to replace her or part them in their bond. I just could not understand why she was the only one of his two sisters who had such an issue with me. Xavier and I tried to fight through all of the obstacles that were against us, but two broken people cannot help or heal one another. We would only continue to put our past hurts on one another and eventually it would come to an ugly head.

He continued to work 14 and 16-hour shifts and my meager earnings from the day care and later the local school system barely made ends meet. It killed me to watch him struggle and I continued to feel like a burden. He was acting different and I knew something was up. There were long distance calls on our phone bill that I couldn't account for; he began criticizing my weight and appearance. It was her, his first love, Shay; he was reaching out to her and planning a Thanksgiving rendezvous. I called the number and typical of the "sideline", she spilled out all the content of their many conversations and told me of their planned rendezvous.

I decided to confront him, and as always, never losing composure, he ignored me. "Xavier, I know you hear me!" I screamed in the master bathroom. "Why in the hell are you calling this trifling hoe? You said she cheated on you and broke your heart and you never wanted to see her again. So why are you trying to meet her for Thanksgiving?" He stood looking into the mirror and focused on shaving himself with the clippers and never said a word. I yelled, "You bastard!, You know what the fuck I am talking about!". He still kept shaving and looking in the mirror to check his work.

His 6'2 caramel frame towered over me and he turned around, looked at me frowned and turned back to the mirror to brush his goatee. Now, I don't take kindly to being ignored. There is something about being ignored so much and so often in my childhood that makes it unacceptable in adulthood for me. He then started the clippers up and I angrily snatched them. The clippers fell out of his hand and across his white tee down the side of his right arm leaving a small scratch. In a flash he grabbed me and before I knew it, my right arm was dangling from its socket. He only stopped when I yelled "You broke it, you broke my arm!" I was shocked; he had never shown any aggression towards me before but had a look on his face as that of someone possessed and out of control. It scared me to death. I tried swinging back at him with the left arm but I was powerless. He shook me like an old Raggedy Ann doll and threw me onto our bed. I landed and bounced back up; arm still dangling. He stopped and looked at my arm. I said, "It's broken, you broke my arm". He said, "I have to take you to the hospital". I said, "No, they are going to arrest you". He hunched his shoulders and began to cry as he led me out of the house, into the garage and to the car.

The drive to the hospital was silent. The doctors and nurses who treated me called the police. They kept asking, "Mrs. Grey, has this happened before?" I kept shaking my head no. I wouldn't talk to them. The nurse was speaking to me about abusive relationships and domestic violence. "Mrs. Grey, you can join a group and get some support and help. Is there anywhere safe you can go? We cannot let him take you back home. The police have asked him to leave the hospital". I began to cry. I lay back on the cold sterile bed and balled up in a fetal position. She left the room to get medicine to calm my nerves. I could hear her and the doctor whispering, "She's still a baby herself. I think this has happened before".

I closed my eyes and pretended to be anywhere but there. How could I have ended up in the same situation as the women I had criticized? Am I an abused woman? Noooo, I thought to myself. Then I cried more. I sat up on my good arm and used the phone in the room to dial Kisa. She would understand. She had been beaten in her past relationships and would not judge me. About 30 minutes later, Kisa picked me up and I stayed with her for one day before I returned home. Why did I go back? Because no one in my family had successful marriages. Because I felt it was a fluke and one time occurrence, and if I left surely they'd take my son. So I made excuses and learned his triggers. Over the years, there would be multiple police calls, several other women, choking, dragging and verbal abuse that I hid from my son and most outsiders.

    I had recently reconnected with, Dazon, a high school friend and we had a lot in common. Dazon was a tall, muscular caramel complexion, half Hispanic half Black man with a voice that was soothing and calming. At the time I was a daycare teacher and he was a single father. His children were in my summer camp class. I turned to him for comfort. That affair made me realize many things about myself and that two wrongs don't make a right. "Payne, you know you deserve better" he would say". "I know but Xavier has had so many people fail him and I can't leave because the church says I have to work it out", I would tell Dazon. He would sigh and shake his head but never seemingly judge me. "I am here for you no matter what", he would always remind me. He was a great friend and comfort at the time. But I was torn between his love and my religious duty as a wife. It tormented me night and day. I eventually broke off the relationship with him because I was trying to 'do right'.

I was confused about what love was and decided that the only pure and truly unconditional love is that between parent and child. But I felt as if my own mother didn't love me so who would? I was so lost damaged, broken, and hopeless.

I admitted my affair to Xavier and forgave him for his as well. We decided to embark upon rededicating ourselves to church. Xavier did dedicate his life to the Lord, became a prayer counselor at our church and seemed devout. That lasted for about a year and then something in him changed. I am still unsure what changed him but he changed. He became angry, distant and the verbal abuse was intolerable. I can still hear his words today; no one should ever hear those words. He would say things like, "You're fat". Or "Hey Payne, they have fat burners on sale". And "I am not attracted to you anymore". He would also say, "If it weren't for me, you and Bean would be nowhere, you would have nothing". I never responded to these abusive words. I only cried and continued to eat to mask the pain. I cried a lot. I hated myself and I felt trapped. I spent years in counseling and therapy ALONE because I was the only one who was fighting for the marriage, trying to honor God's word and in essence, save face. I have a hard time with failure and this would be the one thing I failed at in my life. I blamed myself for years, for the weight, for the impatience, for not making enough money and being me. Later I would find unconditional love for myself and true love in the most unexpected place.

I would eventually become single again after an 18-year relationship with Xavier, which would be laughable because I was totally unprepared for the new dating scene. I have had two relationships since the divorce. Xavier has remarried and has a new family. We only interact regarding Bean but I remain very close with some of his family members. Everyone is dating online via several sites, sharing dudes knowingly, and conversations are all via text. And I fell hard. I have found that dating is dangerous and full of trickery and foolishness these days. It is not my experience alone, but that of many women I know. These are not the men of our grandparents' generation. The men who do an honest day's work, take care of their families, understand discretion/home first, and that HIV is real. I wished that I could end this with a true love comes kind of story. But it does, true SELF love.

THE OTHER SIDE OF THRU BY PAYNE NICKERSON

Chapter 3
Friends & Family

Iron sharpens iron
Proverbs 27:17

"Look!" I yelled to my sisters, Kisa and Vashti. Kisa yanked my arm and said to me and Vashti, "You better not stop! Keep walking." I grabbed her hand with my smaller kindergarten hand and began to cry. Kisa said, "Stop crying all the time! Keep walking." I used my free hand to wipe my tears away. We trotted down the long Decatur street trying to figure out where to go. As we walked past our evicted furniture, toys, clothes and belongings, I tried not to turn around and look. But watching the other kids run and grab our things and take them home was heartbreaking. Hearing the kids behind us laughing and saying, "Oooh, somebody got put out", was tormenting. It is the first time I can remember ever feeling embarrassed and ashamed. Vashti and Kisa stopped near the Pizza Hut and I said, "I'm tired of walking". I began to whine and cry. It was hot and my little legs were weary and my book bag seemingly got heavier.

Vashti said, "We need a phone to call mom and daddy." Kisa agreed. We then walked to the rental office and asked them if we could use the phone. I sat in silence until Vashti came back and said, "Daddy said don't move, he is coming". I sat there looking around the leasing office at the busy ladies who were dressed nicely and taking care of business as if nothing different was happening. We were homeless and the day-to-day business was going on without any one being concerned. We sat there in silence until my father walked through the door. I ran up to him and hugged his leg as hard as I could. My father stood at a

tall 6 foot 6 frame and was handsome, caring and a straight shooter. As I hugged his leg, he picked me up and went inside of the rental office. He handed the lady a wad of money and she gave him keys.
He told his best friend Charlie to take us to Burger King to get something to eat and we left.

When we returned, we were living in a new apartment in the same complex. My father had salvaged most of our furniture. I do not recall where my mother was at the time (probably at work) but I remember my sisters being my saving grace and my dad being there. Eventually my parents split and I was broken, I always felt unwanted by my mother. Oftentimes when we were struggling and my father was no longer around she was tired, overworked, underpaid and trying to raise three girls. She would remind me "The doctors told me not to have any more kids and I still had you. After I lost that last baby, I was not supposed to have any more kids". I would just stand there and say nothing as this was repeated to me quite a bit throughout my life. I tried very hard not to be in the way or a bother. I tried to be invisible. I felt invisible. She was proud of my academic accomplishments, never missed a band or orchestra performance, never missed a coronation or homecoming but I still felt unwanted, not liked and never quite good enough.

I was sad a lot and spent days in my room wanting a hug, to be told I was beautiful and to know that I am good enough. I wanted to be a blessing to her and for her to be proud of me. I began to 'perform' for her love and attention. I thought if I made her proud then she would love me. But my sisters seemingly loved me for no reason at all, sure we all teased and joked with one another but deep down, I *knew* they loved me.

From childhood to adulthood my sisters would prove to be my defenders against outsiders and sometimes amongst the sisters. When family members said I'd be nothing because I was pregnant so young, they were there. When my son's father said I didn't come from shit and was never going to be shit, they were there. When my husband flipped between being madly in love with me and hating the sight of me, they were there. I would learn the lesson from them about unconditional love. Each of us have flaws but if you bother one, you have to deal with us all (Candler Rd ALL DAY). And together we raise hell.

They helped me parent, caught the slack when I was in trouble, stood with me through persecution and court battles with my sons father, and gave money when my husband left and we struggled. They were there unconditionally, each giving a part and each being a mother of sorts. Often crying and helping me hide scars, they were there. In the end, when I decided to return to college, they were there, loud and proud. Each of them are distinctive and have played a major role in my life:

Sabrina is the eldest; she has a sensitive heart and is very mysterious. She oftentimes gives me advice and has always found delight in my quick wit as a young girl. She encourages my more creative side and has had unwavering faith in my ability to be successful. She is the perfectionist who doesn't realize that she is perfect how she is, how God made her.

Liz is the strongest of us all. Life had not been kind to her but she is the kindest of all of my sisters. She is known for her ability to put you in your place quickly and without apology. Her giving heart and sweet disposition wins the affection of many but most know not to cross her. Growing up I remember her always making sure we went to school, ate, did our homework and attending parent conferences in place of my mother. She is the protector.

Kisa is the most independent of us all. She was the trendsetter and always worked hard. She left home early to escape the madness that was our normalcy. I admire her strength to overcome several abusive relationships and still love hard. She was my rock when my son was a newborn and daycare was out of the question. She cared for him as her own and was my "mom" for many years. She is the provider.

Vashti is the "I'm going to tell you and get you straight" sister, devout Christian and all of our conscience. She was our moral compass. She always helped with my homework, protected me from bullies, and got on my case at any time. Amazingly her opinion mattered to me more than anyone else. I used to live for her approval. I admired her for being the first to go to college. She is the pathfinder.

As individuals, we are independent and strong but if we could get past a lot of the sisterly BS, all five of us could be as strong as a fist. At this point, we had all been battered by life and trying to find our way through what we learned as little girls, FAITH. We are praying and protective women.

I won't write much more about my sisters except, that I love them. Lord knows we all have our own stories and their stories are just that, theirs. They are women who do much with very little and try hard not to complain. They are mothers who struggle through motherhood without a manual, like most of us. They are aunts who adore their nephew and have been there for him in ways I cannot measure in word. They are sisters who have mothered me, been my friend and been my voice of reason and for all of those reasons I am grateful. In the end, when I decided to return to college to finish what I started, they were there, I love each of them.

There are some sisters that are not born into your family but as your friend they have made themselves like sisters through love, words and deed. I have been blessed to have some friends who are just that, true friends. They are supportive unconditionally through all of my decisions, accomplishments and choices. These women have been strategically placed in my life at various points when God knew I needed more sister friends.

The things that they have watched, endured and stood by me through are unimaginable. They have been my biggest cheerleaders and encouraged the writing of this book to share this journey. Through them I have learned the art of patience, the meaning of silver linings, and countless lessons of remaining positive and focused. All sisters are not by blood, some are through experience. I am grateful for having both. Growing up, you always hear about angels watching over you. I can honestly say I have met my angels.

THE OTHER SIDE OF THRU BY PAYNE NICKERSON

Chapter 4
Sojourning to find MY truth

Truth is powerful and it prevails
Sojourner Truth

I began feeling more like a burden than a wife to Xavier. Feeling like I was not contributing to my household enough, I realized that I needed to return to school and complete my degree in order to be a better mom and wife. I thought maybe my husband would be nicer and not so stressed if I brought more money in. It would be later that I'd find it was the opposite.

I returned to college in Spring 2000 as a sophomore at a well-endowed, prestigious women's college in Georgia. It was there that I learned about oppression of women and patriarchal viewpoints. It was there that

I re-actualized my academic promise and potential. My mentors, two black female professors in the history and sociology department, were great examples and often encouraged me to do more, be more. I was an active scholar and although non-traditional, it was there that I made lifelong friends who supported me through the hell to come.

Upon graduating *cum laude* at age 28 with a bachelor's degree in Africana Studies, I entered into graduate school at a renowned historically black college and university (HBCU). It was there that my passion for social justice flourished as I was mentored and trained by some of the best professionals in my industry. During my matriculation, I was blessed with the opportunity through a 'bridges' program to encourage and train minorities to pursue doctorates. I received additional training at one of the top schools in the country and made lifelong connections there as well. I was blessed beyond measure and excited to be making my way towards my dreams. It was an eye opening experience regarding the promises of a future in social justice and a definite way to positively impact people's lives. Finally, I had 'hooked up' to my purpose.

I was exhilarated and my husband seemed supportive of my bright future. Part of my training required coursework and additional statistical training at another college, so in the summer of 2003 I ventured north and into my future. Was I concerned about my marriage? Of course, there had been inklings of romantic intentions with some of his female friends but words he spoke to me in a heated argument rang in my ear and propelled me to do more. "If it weren't for me, y'all wouldn't have shit, you'd be homeless". Had I become the women I had judged? Dependent?

Stuck? Not able to survive without a man? I began to resent him but more so myself for what I had become.

While completing the summer program, the marriage deteriorated. Missed calls, unable to reach him at night, a myriad of accusations to deflect from his own indiscretions, and of course the ever so famous unanswered I love you. "I have been calling you", he said. I held the phone and checked my nails against the sunset to see if I needed a fill-in. I sucked my teeth as he went on and on. "Where you been? I called you a few times", he said. I rolled my eyes and checked my braids in the mirror. "Studying", I replied. "See how you act? What you been up there doing?" he said. "Xavier, what do you want? I have a late study session to go to and I am going to be late," I responded. He could tell by my tone and nonchalant attitude that I was pissed and he feared my cheating again. "I'm going to come see you soon" he stated. Again, I rolled my eyes and sucked my teeth. I knew he was just coming to scope the layout and see what was really up. I had stopped calling and texting daily. I started ignoring his calls. He visited one weekend in July, after I'd sent my stipend check home to help with bills. He seemed distant and distracted; he hid his cell phone and often took it to the bathroom with him. I feigned ignorance for the sake of peace.

Upon his departure, he said, "I'll call you on the drive back". I smiled and said, "Ok". I had three weeks left in the program. We hugged and gave a quick peck on the lips; he got into his rental car and headed south back to Atlanta. Things went back to how they were before the visit. It was a 10 hour drive and he did not answer my calls the entire ride back. I left a message, "I called. Hope you are safe and call me back when you can". I was more focused and determined than ever to get on my own feet and get my life together.

I returned home in early August to an attitude and further distance. My son and I were left out of his family gatherings, often ignored. The marriage was strained. And the fact that we had no biological children of our own was a constant source of pain for us both. I had lost a baby the year before. My matriculation in graduate school ended well with numerous accolades, awards and acceptance and full 'rides' to some of the best doctoral programs in the country; however I chose my graduate program based upon its reputation, the overall package and its proximity to Georgia (in an effort to save a marriage that was clearly on life support).

Xavier was included in all of my decisions about school. The plan was for my son and I to go ahead and establish roots in another small southern city and he would follow. We would rent out our home in Georgia until we returned. He would attend graduate school there as well. Needless to say, he never showed and I began to fall apart. I began to receive disturbing calls. In the midst of my doctoral comprehensive exams and dissertation proposal defense preparation, friends of mine began consistently calling.

"Hello", I answered. "Hey lady, I was just checking on you" said my friend Reine. "What's up lady?" I responded. "Girl, nothing much been hanging out a lot with my sister and her friends and going to lots of concerts and stuff" replied Reine. "When are you coming back to the A?" she asked. "It'll be a while, at least a year", I replied. There was a thoughtful but pregnant pause and she said, "Does Xavier have a sister?" "Yes, he has two sisters. Why?" I replied. She then explained that she had seen him at several events around town with a short dark skinned girl. Part of the description fit one of his sisters; however, it was highly unlikely that she would be with him drinking and attending secular music concerts. I immediately excused myself from the call. I began to try and reach him.

In his usual fashion, there were additional unanswered texts and calls. His visits became fewer and fewer. Then I learned about Angie, April, Kathy, Bridgette, Sheila, and Sasha - to name a few. I busied myself with being a good mother and student. By now, my son was standing well over 6 feet and in high school. He was the mirror image of my father and a very bright and talented student. I had aged and was having some health issues tied to my high levels of stress. But I was still in tune enough to recognize that my son was unhappy there and the educational system was not conducive to what I desired for him. So I agreed with his grandfather to send him home to Atlanta to go to school. He would live with his grandparents until I returned. He moved back in December 2004 and I was devastated, lonely and getting sick.

Tensions between me and Xavier were mounting and by March 2005, my husband filed for divorce citing irreconcilable differences. He visited and said, "You are here doing your thing and you put this all before me and left me in Atlanta so what was I to do?" I replied, "Have some patience, come here, or learn to work through this. I don't have much time left here". He shook his head and said sternly, "I don't want this or you anymore. We married young. I am missing out on things in my life and I put my life on hold to marry you and help you raise your son". I was aghast, it was the first time he'd ever referred to Bean as 'my son'. Imagine that! I'd been sending home loan and earning monies to help with the bills. I was devastated. Before leaving, he asked me for my keys to our suburban home and said that his attorney would contact me. I asked him if he thought that counseling would help or if we could try legal separation before divorce. His lips said, "Yes" but his eyes told me he wasn't going to go for it. He was totally out of the marriage and completely done. I could see it in his face.

    I did what I have always done, I sought out the church and was told to pray and fight for my marriage. I did. I refused to sign the papers and purposed myself to drive to Atlanta Wednesdays after class and stay until Monday mornings at 5am and then drive back to school. I began to lose weight, my hair was noticeably falling out. I begged him to stay, to try. I couldn't fail at this too. Nothing changed.

In the Summer of 2005, I passed my doctoral qualifying exams and began preparing my dissertation. As I prepared to defend my proposal, I found out he was still dealing with one particular lady and I called her. Why? Because I needed to know the truth. She, also married, was more than happy to share the details of their 'friendship'. He was enjoying concerts, dates and dinners with her. Things he always complained we couldn't do because we were strained for money.

November 2005 marked our 12th wedding anniversary; he was supposed to visit to celebrate. No call. No show. It was a three hour ride so I drove to Atlanta that night. As I pulled up a car was in the driveway, the garage door up. It's my home, so I walked in and up the stairs. I heard laughter and music. They were in our bedroom, sitting on our bed, his shirt open sipping on Hennessy. I was in pure shock! I yelled, "Who the hell are you?" as I lunged for her. She smiled. He leapt to his feet and grabbed me by my arms yelling, "What are you doing here!!" He yelled to her "Call the police!"

I was in pure shock and screaming as he drug me down the first flight and second flight of stairs of our two story home. Then out the garage door where he pushed me towards my silver Lancer and said, "Leave, you have no business here. I don't want you". I cried and tried my best to get back into the house. With each step, he pushed me back towards my car and yelled, "Leave!!" He then started laughing uncontrollably; I flew into a fit of rage and started swinging on him, missing each time. He grabbed me by my throat and pinned me to my car and said, "Get out of here". I bit him.

I went in my trunk to get my tennis racket to bust the windows out her car. I was thinking, she'd have to explain that when she got home. I turned to hear him say, "Yes, I have a disturbance in my home the address is...." I just shook my head. I stayed and didn't run. I was not the person in the wrong here. I dialed, "Hello" the male voice on the other end of the phone answered. I said, "Hi, Norman is Kai home?" "No", he responded and went on to ask, "Why are you crying? What's going on?" I then explained the evening's events. He said, "Leave, get out of there". I could not believe my ears but I was not leaving. I responded, "Please ask Kai to call me back" and hung up the phone.

Within ten minutes Kai arrived at our home and was stepping in between us fighting. Finally all the things he said I'd been lying about (women, drinking and fighting) could be proven. She asked, "Xavier, who is the lady in the house?" He replied, "My friend and Payne has no business here, I don't want her". She looked at me and said, "Do you hear him? Remember he said this". She turned to him and asked, "Have you been drinking?" He laughed and then turned towards the house to look up in the window and see his friend peeking out. Finally the police arrived and this drunken man said, "It's over I don't want her and my friend is inside". After the whole story came out, they made Xavier's friend leave. They made me stand across the street until they calmed him down. I went home with his sister, Kai, afraid of what my family would do to him.

I called Vashti and told her, I couldn't face my mother. The next afternoon I knew it was bad when I showed up at Vashti's house and her best friend Veronica began to tend to my wounds. I took my shirt off and Vashti began to cry as Veronica rubbed essence oils on my bruises. They both began to pray. I couldn't deal; I was defending my dissertation proposal the next day. So I drove back to school, put on long sleeves and lied about the visible bruises and scratches. I passed the dissertation proposal with flying colors but was failing in life.

Over the next few months I developed stress related psoriasis of the scalp and my hair was visibly thinning. I began to fast and pray more. I talked to my son every day and saw him whenever I came into town. I was determined to finish and I did. I returned to Atlanta and moved back home but trust was broken and I was afraid. I was afraid I'd flip at any given moment out of fear. We got along enough to parent and participate in my son's activities and help him through the college application process. My son graduated with honors and both families were proud and present. We all sat together in celebration of him and my son's uncle said, "He's grown now there's no reason for you to be here". I knew what he meant. How did he know? How could he know? I gave him a knowing nod.

July rolled around and my husband went out to a club and came home and said, "I am leaving, I need my own space and this still isn't working for me". I just looked at him in awe. I asked, "Where are you going?" He replied, "I am moving in with a friend". I knew from that statement that he was gone. He moved in with a female friend for four days. My son and I spent the fourth of July with his family as by this time, although my family and friends loved me dearly; they were tired and waiting for me to get tired. His younger sister, who hadn't cared much for me in the beginning and seemed to dote on him stated, "Girl how long you gonna do this? Oooooh, Get a backbone or something." I said, "What do you mean?" She said, "My brother only does you like that because you allow it and you won't stand up for yourself. He's become so disrespectful and he doesn't even try to hide what he does any more". I got quiet.

I began to think and plan after that conversation. In August we took my son to college and I knew I had to leave because nothing had changed, he was still angry at me about school, my son had pointed out that he knew his stepdad was 'sleeping' with his customers and also said that it was all too much. I could hear my heartbreaking. So I plotted my escape. Xavier left one

Saturday morning and I moved while he was at work. He returned to an empty house and had no idea where to find me.

Months passed and we were cordial off and on but separated. I missed companionship and feared being alone but not enough to go back. He was dating and met his new love on a skiing trip, she was *everything* opposite of me. I continued working on my dissertation and graduated December 2007 with my Ph.D. Ironically, my research was reflective of my own life issues and circumstances. During my matriculation and divorce, I had several health challenges and surgeries. The more literature I reviewed the more I grew stronger and more confident, less dependent and less afraid. My relationship with God, not the church, grew at this time. I began praying and fasting more. I became more spiritual and less religious. I was truly being born again in every sense of the word. Every day I prayed for him, myself and my son. I would soon see that there is freedom in forgiveness.

THE OTHER SIDE OF THRU BY PAYNE NICKERSON

Chapter 5
Freedom in Forgiveness

"The three hardest things to do are: to trust, to have faith, and to forgive" - Jane Fonda's character Georgia, in the movie Georgia Rule

As I began to read my Bible more there was one thing that stuck out - forgiveness. I had to forgive everyone and everything. I wrote letters to everyone that ever hurt me. The letters allowed me to get it all out; however I burned them, as not to cause conflict or have them face the things they would categorically deny. To forgive, is not just saying so and moving along unscathed, it is a process and takes time. True forgiveness is work, but it's worth it.

THE OTHER SIDE OF THRU BY PAYNE NICKERSON

I had to forgive my parents for neglecting and not protecting me from being abused. I forgave every man in my life that hurt and disappointed me and made me hate being a woman or anything feminine. I had to forgive. The people who hurt me were living their lives and I was stuck in bitterness and anger. One thing I do know is that bitterness will eat you alive like a cancer and kill your spirit. The hardest thing was not forgiving but asking forgiveness. I had to do it. I had to ask my son to forgive me for several things:

-Being an ill-equipped mom and fumbling through parenthood

-Bringing men into his life who constantly disappointed and rejected him (his father and my ex-husband)

-Being an angry and frustrated mother who often took it out on him

So I wrote him this letter:

My Dearest Sun,

You are indeed a blessing and my greatest accomplishment. Many times in life I have cried because I feel that I have failed you. When I watch you stumble and try to find your way as a man in this cruel and calculating world, I feel responsible. I feel responsible for not making the best choices in role models in the men that have been in your life. I oftentimes feel as if I have failed parenting because of the hardships you have endured because of my choice to become a parent at such a young age. Sun, kids do not come with handbooks or guidelines and we do the best we can as parents.

THE OTHER SIDE OF THRU BY PAYNE NICKERSON

In my life I have made many judgments of my own parents and sometimes those judgments have come back to haunt me and I have made some of those the same mistakes in our lives. I have done the best I can with what I was given. Everything in my life since you have graced this earth has been for your betterment. But I realize that I have not always managed life's pressures well. Oftentimes taking my anger and frustration out on you and being very hard on you regarding expectations. You should have played more; you should have had a happier childhood. As your mother I knew what the world had in store for you and was determined that neither you nor I would be another statistic. I was determined to emphasize education, speaking well and responsibility.

Perhaps I loved you too much and too hard. Perhaps I tried too hard to protect you from the abuse I suffered and from ill meaning people and that may

have crushed your more creative side. For these reasons I owe you an apology and ask your full forgiveness for hurting you, disappointing you and failing you. Over all, I have done the best I could with what we were given and I think that you are a great young man that is destined for more. Your life is a blessing as you have been near death three times before the age of 22 and God keeps mercifully saving you. You have a purpose, you have promise and you have power – embrace it. Forgive everyone, everything. I love you more than life itself.
Always, Mom.

I have written this in letter, in text and said it to him via phone call on multiple occasions. His response is always the same, no matter what channel of communication, "No worries, Mom. I love you. It's okay and I understand". We remain closer than ever and have a great mutually respectful relationship. His friends often admire and some envy our relationship. I have adopted them all as my children. Bean is becoming a great man and I am blessed that God entrusted me with his life and care. I am blessed that my mother, my sisters, and his father's parents were the village that helped me to raise him and provide for him. I always say, he is my greatest gift and accomplishment. He saved my life.

THE OTHER SIDE OF THRU BY PAYNE NICKERSON

Chapter 6
Accepting the Gift of Goodbye

You've got to know when it's over. Let me tell you something. I've got the gift of good-bye. It's the tenth spiritual gift, I believe in good-bye. It's not that I'm hateful, it's that I'm faithful, and I know whatever God means for me to have He'll give it to me. And if it takes too much sweat I don't need it. Stop begging people to stay.
-TD Jakes, December 2010

During the period of separation from my husband I found solace in prayer and fasting. I desired to be on a better and more fruitful path. For the first time in life, I believed I could have it all. I *deserved* to have it all. One morning I was getting dressed for work and turned the television on, Dr. Creflo Dollar was preaching the message, "Accepting the Gift of Goodbye", it moved something in me. I do not nor have I ever attended Pastor Dollar's church but I often watch services of his, TD Jakes, Joyce Myer, and Joel and Victoria Olsteen.

Sometimes in life we hold on to the very thing God is trying to deliver us from. Out of fear, doubt, unbelief, and all the other things that keep us bound. We hold on to that which destroys us out of comfort and familiarity. But this message was different, it literally struck me. It was like a bolt of lightning! I needed to accept that my marriage was over. I'd gone above and beyond to keep my family together, and there was nothing left to fight for. I needed to accept that saying goodbye to a past full of hurt would save me. I needed to accept saying goodbye to the old me and be bold enough to live and love the new me.

Xavier and I had been separated for a while but he invited me to visit our home on Christmas Eve. I stopped by the house and also picked up some mail that had come from the college regarding Bean. "You look nice," he said. "Thanks", I said back to him as we sat on the steps. "What are your holiday plans", I asked him. "The usual", he responded. That meant him floating around to his different family members houses. "Ok, well I have to go to a party at my sister's" I stated as I walked towards the door and he slapped my behind. I just shook my head and laughed. I proceeded to my car and smiled at him and left headed towards the north side of town.

    As I drove away, I smiled at the house with all the Christmas decorations that made us so happy and held so many memories for us. While I was at the party, my text message tone alerted me to a new message. The message read, "You looked really nice. Enjoy the party and I will stop by and see Bean before he heads back to college". I smiled at the message and kept partying. During the party, my sister gave me a piece of mail for Xavier so I decided to drop it off to him.

As I pulled up in the driveway behind his car, I shivered because it was cold this Christmas Eve but you could smell the neighborhood fireplaces and I could see the smoke coming from the chimney of the split level home we shared for most of Bean's life. I walked up the three steps to the house and could see two shadows through the beveled glass front door. I rang the bell and he slightly opened the door. His eyes grew big but he was blocking me entering the home. I could see her feet. Her Timberland boots lay scattered on the cream colored living room carpet. I shook my head and said, "Who is that?" He tried using his body to block the door. I just laughed and said, "Does she know I was just here and you were trying to sleep with me?" He laughed and frowned and said, "I don't know what you are talking about". I was taken by complete surprise and said, "Am I not your wife and did you not just spend yesterday at my home chilling with me and Bean? Did you not just ask if we could work it out?" He replied, "I don't know what you are talking about. I am not married. I have never been married." He reached through the door pushed me back, shut it and locked it.

I walked down the stairs in disbelief. I was totally shocked. I returned to my home and sat and looked at my Christmas tree. Bean was a college freshman home on holiday break and visiting with his grandparents until the New Year. The house was lonely but I laid across my sofa and watched all the Christmas classic movies until I fell asleep. *"I've done enough cryin, cryin, cryin…time to do something for me*" I heard my Mary J. Blige ringtone and went rushing for my phone. "Hello", I said as I heard my half-sister Bird say, "Mom and Dad said are you still coming to dinner?" I said, "Yes, I will be there by 1". I got up and got dressed and headed towards my father's house for Christmas. I sat and ate with my father, stepmother and siblings. We then watched movies, played cards and engaged in all of the regular family holiday pastimes. My father was an older thinner version of his younger self but still proud. "Baby girl, I am so proud of you. I want the best for you. Don't take no wooden nickels, remember that, ok?" I responded, "Yes, Dad".

As I left their home that night, I was in deep thought but as the cars rode past me, I saw Xavier in his truck. I wanted to talk to him. I was sure that separation was not enough and he had not changed so his offer of reconciliation was no longer an option. As

I pulled over to the parking lot of the plaza where he'd parked, I notice him and a lady walking towards the drugstore and they stopped in their tracks. He had spotted me. He told her, "Get in the truck". She hurriedly walked to his car. And he got in and sped off. I thought for a split second.

And I took off behind them through the streets of Stone Mountain and Decatur, we were in a true street chase and if I knew him well enough, he was looking for the first police officer he could find. True to his character, he drove straight to the police station and stopped the first officer he could to say, "She is stalking us and following us, please tell her to stop". The police officer came over and said, "This man is saying that you are following him and his girlfriend". I smiled and said, "Sir, I am his wife and that is his girlfriend in the truck. If you can please make out a report for the incidence I would appreciate it". The officer smiled and said, "Mrs, I understand and I also think you should just go home after this". I did a U-turn which put me window to window with Xavier and said, "Thanks". He looked confused. I said, "Knowing you, you would deny all of this so who better to serve as a witness that you admitted to your girlfriend and had her in the car than a police officer". I smiled and rode off into the night. Two days later, I filed for a divorce and it was granted in 90 days.

I had accepted the gift of goodbye. I had freed myself from the guilt of failure, the shame of abuse, the verbal and intermittent physical abuse, and my self-imposed religious obligation. Goodbye was a gift that I needed, wanted and had to get through. I had recently graduated with a doctorate degree and a week later filed for divorce. My life was spinning in the vortex and as I spun the things of old flew off of me and out of my life and spirit. I felt like a lotus flower that had struggled through so much and just wanted to "be". I wanted to be a better me, to make a difference in this world, to no longer be bound by fear and other people's expectations; I wanted to be my best self. I wanted to rise above all of my experiences (good and bad) and to learn the lessons so as not to repeat them. Finally, I was on the other side of thru in so many ways. I was over all I had been thru. I had gone through many things and I was just thru with abuse, self-pity, self-loathing and most of all thru with being a victim.

Chapter 7
Phoenix: And Still I Rise

Out of the huts of history's shame
I rise
Up from a past that's rooted in pain
I rise
I'm a black ocean, leaping and wide,
Welling and swelling I bear in the tide.
Leaving behind nights of terror and fear
I rise
Into a daybreak that's wondrously clear
I rise
Bringing the gifts that my ancestors gave,
I am the dream and the hope of the slave.
I rise
I rise
I rise.
-Maya Angelou, 1978, Still I Rise

I am almost 40 years old and there is still so much more to be written in the life of Payne. I felt compelled to share what I would consider the formative stage of my life so that others may be bold, break barriers and expectations. I am very excited about this next stage of my life as I have checked so many things off my life's "to do" list that I am creating a new one from the hope, faith and love I am surrounded by.

The importance of reading my testament to hope and faith is that you understand and realize that I am not a victim, but a survivor. I know of many women who have survived physical, sexual and emotional abuse by abusing themselves, drugs, alcohol or turning to prostitution or stripping. I have no judgment of them, we all deal with life's challenges in different ways. I have had no substance addictions, have never prostituted or stripped; however I do escape through other means. I bury myself in education, work, reading and reality TV. All of these have provided me an escape.

I, a survivor of abuse on multiple levels, sexual abuse, child abuse, a teen mother, a divorcee, emotional abuse in past relationships and a woman who suffered from a lack of self-love and PTSD, am now an accomplished professional with four degrees. I have a PhD, am a professor, a great mother to an awesome young man and am madly in love, with myself. I am active in the community as a volunteer and mentor. I give of my time and assistance with love and patience. I have recently been inducted into an honor society, became an advisory board member of an international organization, and started my own company.

Some would say I am successful, I say to whom much is given much is required. Some would say my life story is nothing short of a miracle. Some would say that my life is no different from anyone else who grew up in an urban city overrun with poverty, drugs and nihilism. I say it is miraculous, that my faith and hope propelled me to keep dreaming and striving. I say my life is different in that my internal motivation sometimes exceeds my own expectations and is tiring. I say that I have seen things others could only imagine, read about or watch in disbelief. I spend my extra time helping college students, mentoring young women of various socioeconomic statuses, and encouraging women through workshops and health seminars.

Life does have balance. Good does come full circle. Don't give up. When a door closes, a window opens. We hear these things all the time. But I tell you as I sit here writing this last chapter while looking out over the beautiful Pacific Ocean on business in Oahu, Hawaii that I could not imagine the gifts that are given with patience, prayer and perseverance.

I could not imagine having a career that I truly love which makes a difference in the lives of others and is so fulfilling. I could not imagine, having conversations with all of my exes that are not laced with bitterness but with love and compassion for them as humans and in hopes that they get it right. That I could not imagine, having such love for myself, as I hated myself growing up in ways that no one could imagine. And I thought God hated me because I endured so much pain, shame and hate. That I could not imagine, a more wonderful son and that the sisters who cared for me, I am now able to return the favor and make them proud. That I could not imagine, you as beautiful as you are taking the time to read my story. But my deepest prayer is that you KNOW life is balanced and that if you hold on, regardless of what present day may be telling you, a change gone come.

THE OTHER SIDE OF THRU BY PAYNE NICKERSON

~~~~~~~

Our deepest fear is not that we are inadequate.
Our deepest fear is that we are powerful beyond measure.
It is our light, not our darkness that most frightens us.
We ask ourselves, who am I to be brilliant, gorgeous, talented, fabulous? Actually, who are you *not* to be?
You are a child of God.
Your playing small does not serve the world.
There is nothing enlightened about shrinking so that other people won't feel insecure around you.
We are all meant to shine, as children do.
We were born to make manifest the glory of God that is within us.
It's not just in some of us; it's in everyone.
And as we let our own light shine, we unconsciously give other people permission to do the same.
As we are liberated from our own fear, our presence automatically liberates others.
-Marianne Williamson, 1992, *A Return to Love*

THE OTHER SIDE OF THRU BY PAYNE NICKERSON

~~~~~~~

And then the day came,

when the risk

to remain tight

in a bud

was more painful

than the risk

it took

to Blossom.

-Anais Nin, *Risk*

Citations

Angelou, Maya. (1978) "Still I Rise" from *And Still I Rise.* Random House, Inc.

Frost, Robert. (1920) The Road Not Taken. *Mountain Interval.* New York: Henry Holt and Company. Retrieved May 12, 2012 from www.bartleby.com/119/.

Jakes, T.D. (2008). The Gift of Goodbye. Retrieved June 2012 from http://www.tumblr.com/tagged/td%20jakes

Langston, Hughes (1994). Mother to Son. *The Collected Poems of Langston Hughes:*Vintage Books.

Marshall, Gary. (Producer & Director). (2007). *Georgia Rule* [Film]. Los Angeles: Universal Pictures.

Nin, Anais. (n.d.) Risk. As quoted in Living on Purpose : Straight Answers to Universal Questions (2000) by Dan Millman, p. 4

Truth, Sojourner. (n.d.) Truth Prevails. Retrieved May 12, 2012 from http://www.fdff.org/truth-panel-2.html

Williamson, Marianne. (1996). A Return to Love: Reflections on the Principles of A Course in Miracles. Harper Paperback.

www.ingramcontent.com/pod-product-compliance
Lightning Source LLC
Chambersburg PA
CBHW072056290426
44110CB00014B/1706